The XXL Air Fryer Cookbook

Quick and Delicious Air Fryer
Recipes for Family and Friends
incl. Desserts and Snacks

Anthony Parkins

TABLE OF CONTENTS

Introduction

Greasy, oil-drenched fried foods were just the thing back in the day. When we started experiencing poor health linked with these kinds of foods, though, things began to change. Most of us made the switch to other forms of cooking to eat more healthily, such as boiling vegetables and eating lean meats. It wasn't until the air fryer was patented that most of us got back to enjoying crispy, fried food. Fried food was healthier than ever before, and fried food was back in fashion.

As well as making fried food much healthier, this invention also made it much faster. It lets us be more creative and innovative with the recipes we come up with. Moreover, with every household rushing to buy one of these fantastic appliances, we can expect to discover even more fresh, delicious recipes as more families and friends discover the wonders of air-fried food and pass on the good news. Let's find out more.

What is an Air Fryer?

An air fryer is an appliance that gives results which are akin to a deep fryer but with little or no oil used in the cooking process. In recent years, air fryer usage has risen across the globe. Today, you can fry all kinds of dishes, ranging from roasted vegetables to French fries, to souffles and profiteroles.

How do Air Fryers Work?

Surprisingly, an air fryer doesn't work by frying – in the same way a deep fryer does – but it's much more like a hot air convection oven fryer. The food in the air fryer is held by a cooking basket with small holes in it. The fan blows hot air around the food. This creates a convection effect which cooks the food, causing it to become crispy and brown.

The air fryer's internal temperature stays at about 160°C which is sufficient to cook foods that are coated in breadcrumbs such as chicken tenders, or foods which are not coated like classic potato skins. The air fryer cooks things faster than a traditional oven and can distribute heat more evenly compared to many other appliances. Soon, we'll find out which foods you can cook in an air fryer. First, though, let's investigate fat removal technology further.

Types of Air Fryer

Paddle Air Fryer

Paddle air fryers save you the hassle of pulling out the food from the appliance to stir it. They have a paddle inside the air fryer, which moves through the basket to easily circulate the hot air. In most of them, you can remove the paddle while cooking if you think the paddle is getting in the way.

Basket Air Fryer

Basket air fryers cook food in a basket. The basket has holes in it to allow hot air to get through and around your food. You might still need to stir a few times during cooking. You cannot cook saucy dishes with a basket air fryer. They have the advantage of being cheaper than paddle air fryers, but they do need cleaning more often.

Convection Countertop Air Fryer

Countertop convection air fryers heat food via the convection effect. Different models have an air fryer setting which enables you to get similar results to standard air fryers. They offer more versatility and flexibility than other types of air fryers. They are larger but have multiple cooking options to help you try out a broader range of recipes. You can also use the wire racks to cook more than one thing at one time.

Next, let's find out more about the role of fat removal technology.

What is Fat Removal Technology?

Fat removal technology is designed to extract and remove excess fat from your food and capture it. This means you can fry foods using little to no oil. What's more, the accompanying rapid air technology helps ensure you get supremely crispy results every time. This makes it the healthiest possible way to fry food for you, your friends, and your family.

Why choose an XXL Air Fryer and what features does it have?

When you buy an XXL air fryer, you don't just get an appliance you can fry foods with. You can also use your new machine to roast, grill, bake and even re-heat food. In addition, if you choose an XXL family-sized air fryer you can fit a whole chicken inside it if you want to. You can cook up to 6 servings of a meal in one go, which is perfect for families and those who enjoy hosting dinner parties. There are also a number of pre-set cooking programs you can use to make things extra simple.

As if all this wasn't enough, it will also cook food up to 1 ½ times faster than in a traditional oven. It's also often cheaper to use an air fryer than it is to use an oven. Lastly, you can use the 'keep warm' mode so that you can be flexible about your serving times. After the food has been enjoyed, you won't have trouble cleaning up either. Both the air fry basket and the removable drawer have non-stick coating which makes cleaning them quick and easy. Now it's time to talk about which foods you might want to cook up for your family and friends in your air fryer.

Which Foods Can You Cook in an XXL Air Fryer?

When air fryers first came on to the market, many people believed that they were just another appliance you could use to whip a tasty snack and a handy way to re-heat food. But an air fryer is not designed to be used to cook quick, convenient meals alone as this little cookbook will illustrate.

You can cook anything you've ever baked or roasted in an oven faster in an air fryer. This could be anything from pork, steak, chicken breast or breaded foods like chicken tenders. Regardless of whether the food is breaded, the air fryer will cook it at the ideal temperature, so the meat will end up being juicy and tender. Fat gets extracted and captured by the fryer too, so the meals you make will not only be delicious but will also be more healthy than more traditional ways of frying would be.

Do you love your vegetables? Not to worry, if you spray a little olive oil into your air fryer, your vegetables will appear brown, crispy and will be sure to satisfy your cravings. Indeed, most vegetables will cook in an air fryer in around 10 minutes. You can try baked potatoes, mushrooms, broccoli and even asparagus. You will not be disappointed. You could even say that the air fryer is a 'jack of all trades' amongst kitchen appliances. Not only can you cook fresh meat and vegetables that will make your taste buds sing — not to mention those of your friends and family — you can also take frozen foods and taste them in all their air-fried goodness in almost no time at all. Later, we'll explore other benefits you can get from air frying some of your favourite foods. Next, however, let's find out which foods you should avoid cooking with this super versatile appliance.

Foods you Should Never Cook in an Air Fryer?

Before you rush into your kitchen and switch on your shiny new air fryer, a word of caution should be sounded. There are some foods that should never see the inside of an air fryer. Here they are:

- Foods with a wet batter (unless they are frozen or fried beforehand).

  - ❑ Wet batter would create mess and does not crisp up in the same way it would if it were submerged in hot oil. The way to ensure you make supremely crispy foods in an air fryer is to coat it in flour, eggs, and breadcrumbs.

- If you cook fresh greens like spinach in an air fryer, they will cook unevenly because of the speed with which the hot air circulates around the food.

  - ❑ Uneven cooking makes it highly like that leafy greens will burn.

  - ❑ If you want to air fry vegetables, choose ones that have some weight, like zucchini or broccoli.

  - ❑ Frozen vegetables are also more likely to be successful and are less likely to burn because they retain more moisture from the ice.

- Cooking whole roasts can be tricky.

  - Even if the whole roast can fit into the air fryer, as with the XXL, there is a chance that the roast will not cook evenly. The part of the roast nearest to the heat source may burn by the time the part furthest away from it is cooked.

  - If the roast is too large, there may not be enough room for the hot air to circulate around the food to cook it properly.

Benefits of Using an Air Fryer

When air fryers are used properly there are advantages to cooking with them. Here are just a few for you.

- Using an air fryer can help encourage people to lose weight.

  - ❏ If you swap deep frying for air frying, you'll decrease the amount of oil and fats you consume which could help you lose weight.

- Air fryers can be safer to use than deep fat fryers.

  - ❏ Air frying does not involve heating substantial amounts of oil. Thus, they do not pose the same level of risk as using a deep fat fryer does, as there are not copious quantities of scalding oil at risk of splashing or spilling.

  - ❏ Nevertheless, people should still take care when using air fryers and follow instructions to stay safe.

- Fewer dangerous potentially cancer-causing compounds form

  - ❏ Research conducted by the International Agency for Research on cancer has suggested that compounds like acrylamide may be linked to the development of some cancers, including pancreatic, breast and throat (esophageal) cancer.

❑ These compounds are formed in some foods when cooked at a high heat, as then something is deep fried. Switching to air frying could reduce the associated health risks.

Now, let's turn our attention to some disadvantages of cooking with an air fryer.

Drawbacks of Using an Air Fryer

As we've seen, there are several good reasons to cook delicious crowd pleasing and often healthy food at home with an air fryer. However, it is incumbent on us to also consider the chief disadvantages of using this wonderful piece of kit.

- Air frying food does not mean it is certain that you will have a healthy diet.

  - ❑ If you want to maintain a healthy diet, it may be better to limit your total intake of fried food altogether — rather than simply replacing deep fired food with air- fried food.

- Other potentially harmful compounds can still form because of air frying.

  - ❑ Air frying can create heterocyclic amines and polycyclic aromatic hydrocarbons when used to cook meats at hot temperatures.

  - ❑ These chemicals are linked to the development of some cancers. It should be noted that more scientific research needs to be done to work out precisely how the formation of those compounds is related to the development of some cancers.

So, bear in mind that while choosing to air fry food is a healthier alternative to deep frying, it still makes fried food. As such, all the health risks that are commonly associated with fried food still exist — though often to a lesser extent.

Handy Tips for Using an Air Fryer

Now that we've discussed the benefits and risks associated with using air fryers, it's time to impart some tips on how to use one.

We'll begin with some tips on how best to prepare an air fryer before you use it, before moving on to talk about steps to take during and after air frying.

Before air frying

- ❏ When preparing to start, ensure you put your air fryer in the right place in the kitchen. It is best to put it on a level surface and on a heat-resistant worktop. Leave about 5 inches of space behind the fryer, where the exhaust vent is positioned.

- ❏ Preheat the air fryer before you put any food inside. This can be done in as little as 3 minutes by setting the timer.

- ❏ Get some good accessories for your favourite new kitchen appliance. For example, you may want to get a pan which is air fryer save and fits inside the main bit of the fryer itself. You might also want to invest in an aluminum foil sling to make it easy to transfer food in and out of the frying basket. You can make one yourself if you wish, by folding a 2-inch by 24-inch strip of foil. That way, when you hold the ends, you can lower the pan into the frying basket and lift the basket out again in the same fashion.

❑ It is also helpful to perfect the best breading technique before you start using the XXL air fryer as you will need to do this for a lot of recipes. When breading foods, always make sure that you coat it well with flour first before dipping it in egg and then the breadcrumbs. If there is only a loose coating of breadcrumbs there is a chance that the fan inside the air fryer will blow the coating off. Press the breadcrumbs firmly onto the food to prevent this from happening.

When frying

❑ Put some water into the cooking drawer of you are cooking bacon or sausage to avoid the grease overheating or smoking.

❑ To ensure even cooking, try not to overcrowd the frying basket. For the best results, there needs to be enough space between the food for hot air to move around it.

❑ Flip food over halfway through the cooking time to make sure both sides go brown and deliciously crispy.

❑ You can safely open your air fryer to check if the food is ready. It does not interrupt the cooking process and the fryer will usually continue cooking from where it left off when you close the fryer again.

❑ One more tip to ensure even cooking is to periodically shake the basket when frying to move the food around.

After frying

- ❑ When you're certain the food is fully cooked, remove the air fryer basket from the drawer before turning out the food.

- ❑ Turning the basket upside down when it is still locked into the fryer will mean the rendered fat will end up on the plate with the tasty air fried goodies.

- ❑ Juices which have collected in the drawer of the air fryer may include marinades which could be used to make a sauce more flavorful. For these reasons, don't dump the contents of the drawer down the sink too hastily. Even if a marinade is greasy, you could still reduce it in a saucepan to achieve the same effect.

Now seems the ideal time to include some fryer cleaning tips before we dig into the scrumptious recipes this little cookbook offers.

How to Clean an Air Fryer

Obviously, even though air frying is a much healthier way to fry food, your appliance is going to need cleaning from time to time. There is, after all, only so much good old soap, water and elbow grease can do to take on stubborn baked-on grease.

With that in mind, here are some tips for you.

- ❑ Unplug your air fryer and let it cool before you start to clean it. To speed up the cooling process you can remove the cooking basket and pan.

- ❑ Wipe the outside surfaces of the fryer by mixing some all-purpose cleaner in with some water in a spray bottle.

- ❑ Spray it on a clean cloth and wipe the outside surfaces. Clean the inside surface of the main unit by spraying the undiluted all-purpose cleaner on another clean cloth and wiping the interior.

- ❑ Clean the coil by wiping down the heating element with the pure all-purpose cleaner to remove oil, stains, or residue with the clean, damp cloth.

- ❑ Wash the pans, tray, and cooking basket by hand or in a dishwasher, if they are dishwasher safe.

- ❑ Get rid of baked-on grease from separate of the machine parts by mixing some all-purpose cleaner with hot water in the sink then and soaking them for about 10 minutes. Then scrub the stains, grease, and residue off the parts with a brush, before drying them thoroughly and putting them back into the component of the air fryer.

At last, you're ready to cook up some more devilishly good air fried foods for your whole family.

Now that you know a little more about how air fryers work and what culinary masterpieces you can conjure up with them, you must be ready to discover some wonderful, simple recipes to start you off on your very own air fryer adventures.

Without further ado, let's dive in!

All the recipes that follow are simple to prepare, so that you are sure to be munching happily away in short order. That's great news for all your friends and family but supurb news for you, too.

Main Meals

Want to impress family and friends with your prowess with the XXL air fryer? Below, you'll find a great variety of tasty, appetizing main meals that you can create with this amazing machine. Is your mouth watering already? Soon, you'll be able to treat guests to a fabulous banquet filled with gorgeous air-fried food.

Let's find a seat a the table right away!

BAKED POTATOS WITH CHORIZO

SERVES 6. CALORIES – 150, FAT – 5G. PROTEIN – 5G, CARBS - 21G
PREP TIME: 5 MINUTES. COOKING TIME: 25 MINUTES.

INGREDIENTS

- 6 potatoes
- 1 red onion
- ½ red / bell pepper
- 100g / 3.5 oz. peas (frozen or fresh)
- 6 slices chorizo
- 1 tbsp sour cream
- 1 tbsp chives (optional)
- Season to taste (salt and pepper)

METHOD

1. Preheat the air fryer to 200°C / 392°F

2. Wash the potatoes well and make sure the skin is clean, then dry with kitchen paper

3. Place potatoes in the basket of the air fryer. Put the basket in the air fryer and set the timer for 25 minutes

4. While waiting, finely chop the red onion

5. Slice the chorizo and red pepper into bite-sized pieces

6. Boil the peas until cooked, usually takes a few minutes

7. When the timer goes off, set the potatoes aside until they cool enough for you to touch

8. Cut the top of each potato when cool enough and scoop out the fluffy insides using a fork

9. Gently put the fluffy insides into a bowl

10. Add the sour cream to the bowl and mash together with the potato

11. Mix in the chorizo, peas, chives , red pepper and peas and season to taste

12. Fill the potato skins with the tasty mixture and serve

PORK SATAY WITH PEANUT SAUCE

SERVES 4. CALORIES - 360, FAT - 22G, PROTEIN – 21G, CARBS - 23G
PREP TIME: 35 MINUTES. COOKING TIME: 10 MINUTES.

INGREDIENTS

- 400g / 14 oz. pork, in 3cm cubes
- 2 crushed cloves of garlic
- 1 shallot, diced or finely chopped
- 1 tsp ginger powder or 2cm of chopped ginger root
- 2 tsp chili paste
- 1 tsp ground coriander
- 2-3 tbsp soy sauce
- 2 tbsp vegetable oil
- 100g / 3.5 oz. peanuts (unsalted and ground)
- 200mg/0.007 oz. coconut milk

METHOD

1. Mix 1 of the crushed garlic cloves with the ginger, 1 tablespoon of soy sauce, 1 tablespoon of oil and 1 teaspoon of chili paste

2. Add the pork and ensure its well covered in the mixture

3. Leave the meat to marinate for 15 minutes

4. Preheat the air fryer to 200°C / 392°F

5. Put the now marinated pork in the air fryer

6. Set the timer for 12 minutes and roast until its brown, remembering to turn the meat once while it's roasting

7. Meanwhile, you can make the sauce

8. Heat 1 tablespoon of oil, add the shallot and gently fry it with the remaining garlic clove

9. Add the coriander / cilantro and fry a little more

10. Mix the peanuts and coconut milk together with 1 teaspoon of chili paste and 1 tablespoon of soy sauce

11. Add in the shallot mixture and boil for around 5 minutes, stirring as needed. If the sauce becomes too thick, add a little water to thin it down

12. Season to taste with soy sauce and hot sauce

ROASTED LAMB RACK WITH MACADAMIA NUT CRUST

SERVES 4. CALORIES – 435, FAT - 36G, PROTEIN - 26G, CARB - 2G
PREP TIME: 10 MINS. COOKING TIME: 30 MINS.

INGREDIENTS

- 800g / 1.7 lb. rack of lamb
- 1 clove garlic
- 1 tbsp olive oil
- pepper & salt
- 75g /2.6 oz. macadamia nuts (unsalted)
- 1 tbsp breadcrumbs (for best results use homemade breadcrumbs)
- 1 egg
- 1 tbsp chopped fresh rosemary

METHOD

1. Chop the garlic finely

2. Mix it with the olive oil to make garlic oil. Brush the rack of lamb the garlic oil and season with salt and pepper

3. Preheat the air fryer to 100°C / 212°F

4. Finely chop the macadamia nuts and place them into a bowl

5. Stir in the rosemary and breadcrumbs

6. Whisk the egg in a separate bowl

7. Coat the lamb by first dipping the meat into the egg mixture, draining off the excess. The coat the meat with the macadamia crust

8. Put the coated lamb in the basket of the air fryer and slide it in

9. Set the timer for 25 minutes

10. When the timer goes off, up the temperature to 200°C / 392°F and set the timer for a further 5 minutes

11. Remove the meat, cover it with aluminum foil and leave it to rest for 10 minutes before serving

Serving suggestion: If macadamia nuts aren't to your taste, you can replace them with pistachios or almonds if you prefer.

CHICKEN PARMESAN

SERVES 4. CALORIES - 541, FAT - 18G, PROTEIN – 47G, CARBS – 43G
PREP TIME: 5 MINUTES. COOKING TIME: 10 MINUTES.

INGREDIENTS

- 4 chicken breasts (each approx. 227g / 8 oz.)
- 56g / 1/4 cup of parmesan (shredded)
- 106g / 1 cup of breadcrumbs (Italian Style)
- 2 eggs (whisked)
- 6 tbsp marinara sauce (approx.)
- 100g / 1/2 cup mozzarella cheese

METHOD

1. Preheat air fryer to 180°C / 360°F
2. Cut the chicken breasts in half, lengthwise and trim them (can use food scissors for this if a knife proves tricky)
3. Pound the chicken into thinner pieces of equal thickness
4. Mix together the breadcrumbs and parmesan cheese in a medium-sized bowl
5. Wisk the eggs together in a separate bowl
6. Dip each chicken breast into the egg mixture and then coat them in the breadcrumb mixture
7. Put the chicken breast in a single layer of the air fryer basket
8. Put the chicken pieces in the air fryer, then cook for 6 minutes
9. Turn the chicken pieces over and top with the marinara sauce and mozzarella
10. Air fry for a further 3-4 minutes until the chicken is fully cooked
11. Serve hot

GENERAL TSO'S CHICKEN

SERVES 4. CALORIES - 302, FAT - 13G, PROTEIN – 26G, CARBS – 18G
PREP TIME: 15 MINUTES. COOKING TIME: 20 MINUTES.

INGREDIENTS

- 453g / 1lb. boneless and skinned chicken legs (Cut into small chunks)
- 1 large egg
- 6 tbsp / 1/3 cup + 2tsp corn-starch
- ¼ tsp salt
- ½ tbsp soy sauce
- ¼ tsp white pepper
- 3 tbsp canola oil
- 3-4 chili peppers (chopped)
- 1½ tbsp chopped fresh ginger
- 1½ tbsp chopped garlic
- 6 tbsp chicken stock/broth
- 2 tsp rice vinegar
- 2 tbsp sliced green onion
- 2 tsp sugar
- 1½ tbsp ketchup
- ½ tsp sesame oil
- ½ tsp sesame seeds

METHOD

1. Beat egg into a large bowl, add the chicken and coat well.

2. Mix together 6tbsp / 1/3 cup of corn starch and salt and pepper in a separate bowl

3. Use a fork to transfer the chicken into the corn starch mixture

4. Use spatula coat every piece well.

5. Pre heat air fryer to 204°C / 400 °F

6. Put the chicken in the fryer basket or on the fryer oven racks leaving space between the pieces

7. Cook the battered chick for 12 to 16 minutes, giving it a shake halfway through

8. Let the chicken dry for about 5 minutes

9. if it's still damp on the one side, cook for a further 1-2 minutes

10. Whisk the remaining 2 teaspoons of corn-starch with the stock/broth, the sugar, the rice vinegar, the soy sauce and ketchup

11. Heat the canola oil and chili in a large pan / skillet on medium heat. When it starts sizzling gently, cook for about 30 seconds until fragrant

12. Whisk the corn-starch mixture again and stir into the mixture in a skillet

13. Turn up the heat so it's at a medium to high temperature. Add the now air-fried chicken in when it starts to bubble

14. Stir to coat the meat and cook until the sauce thickens and clings to the chicken, for about 1-2 minutes

15. Take off the heat and stir in one tablespoon of green onion and sesame oil

16. Put it on a plate sprinkle with sesame seeds and the rest of the green onion

SOUTHERN-STYLE CATFISH WITH GREEN BEANS

SERVES 2. CALORIES - 416, FAT – 18G, PROTEIN – 33G, CARBS – 31G
PREP TIME: 0 MINUTES. COOKING TIME: 25 MINUTES.

INGREDIENTS

- 340g / 12 oz. fresh green beans (trimmed)
- Cooking spray
- 1 tsp light brown sugar
- ½ tsp red pepper (crushed)
- 2 catfish fillets (each 170g / 6 oz.)
- Pinch of salt
- 31g / ¼ cup all-purpose flour
- 1 large egg (lightly beaten)
- 35g / 1/3 cup panko breadcrumbs
- ¼ tsp black pepper
- 2 tsp mayonnaise
- 1½ tsp freshly chopped dill
- ¾ tsp dill pickle relish
- ½ tsp apple cider vinegar
- Pinch of granulated sugar
- Wedges of lemon

METHOD

1. Put green beans in a medium-size bowl and liberally spray them with cooking spray

2. Sprinkle in the crushed red pepper and brown sugar, as well as a pinch of salt

3. Put them in the air fryer basket and cook at 204°C / 400°F for about 12 minutes until well browned and tender.

4. Put in a bowl and cover with aluminum foil to keep warm

5. Next, toss the catfish fillets in a coat of all-purpose flour and shake off any excess

6. Dip one piece at a time in the lightly beaten egg to coat

7. Sprinkle on the panko breadcrumbs

8. Press the fish down to ensure an even coat on all sides

9. Put the fish in the air fryer basket and spray with cooking spray

10. Cook the fish at 204°C / 400°F for around 8 minutes, until cooked through and browned

11. Sprinkle evenly with salt and pepper

12. As the fish cooks, whisk the mayonnaise, freshly chopped dill and dill pickle together with the sugar and vinegar in a small bowl

13. Serve the fish and green beans with tartar sauce and lemon wedges

AIR FRIED EMPANADAS

SERVES 2. CALORIES – 343, FAT – 19G, PROTEIN – 17G, CARBS - 25G
PREP TIME: 15 MINUTES. COOKING TIME: 30 MINUTES.

INGREDIENTS

- 1 tbsp of olive oil
- 85g / 3 oz. lean ground beef
- 45g / 1/4 cup chopped white onion
- 85g / 3 oz. mushrooms (finely chopped)
- 2 teaspoons chopped garlic
- 6 pitted green olives, chopped
- 1/4 teaspoon paprika
- 1/4 teaspoon ground cumin
- Pinch of ground cinnamon
- Approx. 75g / 1/2 cup chopped tomatoes
- 8 square dumpling / gyoza wrappers
- 1 large egg, lightly beaten

METHOD

1. Heat the oil in a medium-sized skillet over a medium-high heat

2. Add the beef and onion, to start breaking it up

3. Cook for about 3 minutes until it starts to go brown

4. Add the mushrooms, stir them occasionally and cook for about 6 minutes until they start to go brown

5. Add the olives, garlic, paprika, cumin and cinnamon

6. Cook until the mushrooms are tender and have released most of their liquid (approx. 3 minutes)

7. Add the tomatoes and cook for 1 minute

8. Transfer the filling into a bowl and let it cool for five minutes

9. Place four dumpling / gyoza wrappers on your work surface

10. Put about 1 1/2 tablespoons of filling into the centre of each wrapper

11. Brush the edges of the wrappers with egg, then fold the wrappers over, pinching the edges to seal

12. Repeat this to fill all 8 of the gyoza wrappers

13. Place four empanadas in a single layer in the air fryer basket

14. Cook at 204°C / 400°F for about 7 minutes until they are nicely brown

15. Repeat the process with the 4 other empanadas and serve hot

MARGARITA PIZZA

SERVES 4. CALORIES – 1573, FAT – 54G, PROTEIN – 69G, CARBS - 202G
PREP TIME: 5 MINUTES. COOKING TIME: 8 MINUTES.

INGREDIENTS

- 4 thin pre-prepared and pre-cooked pizza crusts
- 4 Campari tomatoes, sliced
- 12 tbsp pizza sauce
- 20 slices fresh mozzarella
- Fresh basil
- 4 tsp olive oil

METHOD

1. Spread the pizza sauce over the prepared pizza crusts

2. Place the tomato slices on the pizzas, an equal distance away from each other and the edge of the crust

3. Add the mozzarella in between the tomato slices

4. Place in the air fryer basket and cook at 177˚C / 350°F for 5-8 minutes or until the mozzarella has melted

5. Take the pizza(s) out of the fryer, add the fresh basil and drizzle over the olive oil

6. Serve at once

SPICY ROASTED CHICKEN

SERVES 4. CALORIES – 257, FAT – 13G, PROTEIN – 31G, CARBS – 1G
PREP TIME: 5 MINS. COOKING TIME: 20 MINUTES.

INGREDIENTS

- 450g /15.8 oz. chicken breasts or drumsticks
- 2 tbsp red wine vinegar
- 2 tbsp olive oil
- 1 tsp onion powder
- ½ tsp dried thyme
- ½ tsp cumin (ground)
- ½ tsp paprika
- Pinch of black pepper
- Pinch of salt

METHOD

1. Preheat air fryer to 180°C / 356°F

2. Whisk the olive oil, onion powder, red wine vinegar, thyme, cumin and paprika together in a large bowl

3. Put the chicken in a small shallow dish

4. Sprinkle the mixture over the chicken

5. Season it with pepper and salt and toss to ensure a good coating

6. Cover with plastic wrap and leave to marinate for a few minutes

7. Place the marinated chicken in the air fryer basket

8. Cook for 20 minutes and serve at once

TASTY TURKEY MELT SANDWICH

SERVES 4. CALORIES – 294, FAT – 15G, PROTEIN – 16G, CARBS - 25G
PREP TIME: 5 MINUTES. COOKING TIME: 15 MINUTES.

INGREDIENTS

- 4 lean slices turkey
- 8 slices of whole-wheat bread
- 4 slices cheese
- 8 slices tomato

METHOD

1. Preheat air fryer 180°C / 356°F

2. Top each slice of bread with turkey, cheese and tomato slices

3. Make a sandwich by pressing two slices of bread together

4. place the sandwiches inside the air fryer cooking basket for around 10 to 15 minutes, until the cheese has melted, and the sandwich is well-toasted

5. Serve at once

EGGPLANT (AUBERGINE) AND PARMESAN PANINI

SERVES 4. CALORIES – 883, FAT – 58G, PROTEIN – 32G CARBS – 63G
PREP TIME: 25 MINUTES. COOKING TIME: 25 MINUTES.

INGREDIENTS

- 1 medium Aubergine / Eggplant
- 225g / 7.9 oz. mozzarella cheese
- 3 leaves of chopped basil
- 2 slices of bread
- 60g / ½ cup breadcrumbs
- 180g / 1¼ cups tomato sauce
- 60g / ½ cup mayonnaise
- 2 tbsp milk
- 2 tbsp parmesan cheese (grated)
- 2 tsp parsley (dried)
- 1½ tsp garlic
- ½ tsp Italian seasoning
- A pinch of black pepper

METHOD

1. Slice the Aubergine / Eggplant, salt the sides and place them between pieces of kitchen roll / paper

2. Set the slices to one side for 20 minutes

3. Mix the breadcrumbs, garlic, Italian seasoning, onion powder, parsley, pepper, and salt together

4. Whisk the milk and mayonnaise together in a bowl until the mixture is smooth

5. Preheat the air fryer to 200°C / 392°F

6. Brush any excess salt off the Aubergine / Eggplant slices

7. Coat each side of the slices with mayonnaise mixture then dip into the breadcrumb and seasoning mix

8. Place the well-coated slices on a baking tray and spray them with olive oil

9. Air fry the slices for 15 minutes, remembering to turn them over after 7 minutes

10. After cooking the slices, you can begin making the panini

11. Put a good quantity of olive oil on one side of two slices of bread

12. Put the two bread slices on a cutting board with the oiled side facing down

13. Top the two bread slices with about ¼ of the mozzarella and sprinkle in some parmesan cheese.

14. Divide the Aubergine between the panini bread, spreading the cheese evenly on the slices

15. Spread tomato sauce on top of the Aubergine and add the remaining mozzarella and parmesan cheese

16. Sprinkle the basil on the parmesan, then cover it with another slice of bread with the oiled surface facing up to make a sandwich

17. Gently place the sandwich on a preheated panini press or grill

18. Gently press down to evenly toast both sides of the sandwich

19. Grill for 10 minutes or until the cheese has melted and the bread looks well-toasted

DUCK BREAST WITH ROASTED FIG AND POMEGRANATE SYRUP

SERVES 4. CALORIES – 596, FAT – 11G, PROTEIN - 46G, CARBS - 80G
PREP TIME: 10 MINUTES. COOKING TIME: 50 MINUTES.

INGREDIENTS

- 450g / 15.8 oz. duck breast (boneless)
- 6 fresh figs (halved)
- 480ml / 2 cups fresh pomegranate juice
- 2 tbsp of olive oil
- 3 tbsp brown sugar
- 2 tbsp lemon juice
- 1 tsp salt
- ½ tsp of black pepper
- 2 sprigs of thyme

METHOD

1. Make the pomegranate syrup by combining the pomegranate juice with the brown sugar and lemon juice in a medium-sized saucepan
2. Heat the mixture and bring it to boil
3. Then turn down the heat and leave to simmer for 25 minutes until it's thick enough to coat the back of a spoon
4. Preheat the air fryer to 200°C / 392°F
5. Use a sharp knife to score the skin of the duck breast diagonally to render any fat down
6. Make 4 more diagonal slits across the skin in the opposite direction
7. Season the duck breast using the salt and the ground black pepper
8. Put the duck breast with the skin facing up into the air fryer and fry for 10 minutes
9. Turn the duck breast and air fry for a further 5 minutes
10. Flip the duck breast over so that it's skin side up again and air fry it for 1 more minute
11. Move the duck to a chopping board
12. Drizzle olive oil over the figs, season with pepper and salt
13. Put the seasoned figs into the air fryer for 5 minutes
14. Slice the air fried duck breast and drizzle the warm pomegranate syrup over it
15. Garnish with the sprigs of thyme and serve alongside the roasted figs

FALAFEL WITH TAHINI SAUCE

SERVES 6. CALORIES – 60, FAT – 1G, PROTEIN - 3G, CARBS – 10G
PREP TIME: 15 MINUTES. COOKING TIME: 15 MINUTES.

INGREDIENTS

For Falafel

- 800g / 1.7lb. canned chickpeas (drained and rinsed)
- 5g / 0.17 oz. of packed parsley
- 5g / 0.17 oz. coriander / cilantro
- ½ medium sized white onion (cut into quarters)
- 4 garlic cloves
- 1 tsp baking power
- 1 tsp coriander/ cilantro (dried)
- 1 tsp salt
- 1 tsp cumin
- ½ tsp chili flakes

For Tahini Sauce

- 80g / 2.8 oz. tahini
- Juice of ½ lemon
- 3 tbsp water
- A pinch of salt
- A pinch of chili flakes

METHOD

1. Put the onion, cloves of garlic, fresh coriander/cilantro and parsley into a food processor and blend, then scrape the sides as needed

2. Add the drained chickpeas, coriander powder, chili flakes, cumin, baking powder and salt

3. Pulse to break the chickpeas down into chunks and only stop blending when the mixture turns into a paste

4. Season with salt and pepper

5. Take 2 tablespoons of the paste and shape into a ball, not squeezing too hard

6. Do this to make balls with the rest of the paste

7. Place some of the balls into the air fryer and cook for 15 minutes at 190°C / 374°F

8. While the falafels are cooking in batches, you can prepare the tahini sauce

9. Put the tahini and lemon juice in a medium-sized bowl

10. Add water and stir to mix it well, continue adding water as needed until you achieve a good consistency

11. Season to taste with salt and chili flakes

Serving suggestion: You can serve the falafels with the sauce, in a salad or in a pitta bread.

TERIYAKI SALMON

SERVES 2. CALORIES – 276, FAT - 10G, PROTEIN - 29G, CARBS - 13G
PREP TIME: 20 MINUTES. COOKING TIME: 15 MINUTES.

INGREDIENTS

- 180g / 6.3 oz. salmon
- 110g / 3.8 oz. brown sugar
- 4 tbsp soy sauce
- 6 tbsp rice wine vinegar
- 2 garlic cloves (crushed)
- 1 tsp ginger (ground)

METHOD

1. Combine the soy sauce, brown sugar, garlic, ginger, and rice wine vinegar in a pan

2. Heat the teriyaki sauce until the sugar dissolves

3. Marinate the salmon in the teriyaki sauce for at least 20 minutes, but leaving it overnight is best

4. Make a shallow dish out of aluminum foil

5. Put the marinated salmon in the handmade aluminum dish

6. Put the fish into the air fryer basket

7. Slide the basket into the air fryer and cook at 175°C / 347°F for approx. 7 minutes

8. Remove the basket from the air fryer and pour the marinade over it

9. Slide the basket back into the air fryer and cook at the same temperate for a further 7 minutes

KING PRAWNS IN HAM WITH RED PEPPER DIPPING SAUCE

SERVES 4. CALORIES – 317, FAT – 17G, PROTEIN – 42G, CARBS – 6G
PREP TIME: 15 MINUTES. COOKING TIME: 25 MINUTES.

INGREDIENTS

- 10 frozen king prawns (defrosted)
- Tapas fork
- 1 large red bell pepper
- 5 slices of raw ham
- 1 large garlic clove (crushed)
- 1 tbsp olive oil
- ½ tbsp paprika
- ½ tsp black pepper

METHOD

1. Preheat the air fryer to 200°C / 392°F

2. Put the red bell pepper into the air fryer basket and slide it in

3. Set the timer for 10 minutes and roast the red bell pepper until the skin is slightly charred

4. Remove the red pepper and put it in a bowl

5. Cover it with a lid and let it rest for 15 minutes

6. Peel the prawns, remove the black vein at the back

7. Slice into the ham into halves, lengthwise

8. Use the slices to wrap the prawns

9. Coat each ham wrapped prawn in the olive oil and toss them into the fry basket

10. Set the timer to 3 minutes, slide the cooking basket in and cook until the prawns get crispy

11. While the prawns are cooking, remove the red bell pepper from the bowl and peel off the skin

12. Take out the seeds and cut it into pieces

13. Use a blender to puree the red bell pepper with paprika, garlic and some olive oil

14. Pour the blended sauce onto a dish and finish off by seasoning with salt and pepper

15. Serve the ham wrapped prawns on a platter with a tapas fork and the red pepper dipping sauce

MOROCCAN MEATBALLS WITH MINT YOGURT

SERVES 4. CALORIES – 524, FAT – 32G, PROTEIN – 39G, CARBS – 21G
PREP TIME: 5 MINUTES. COOKING TIME: 25 MINUTES.

INGREDIENTS

For Meatballs

- 450g / 15.8 oz. lamb (ground)
- 225g / 7.9 oz. turkey (ground)
- 60ml / ¼ cup of olive oil
- 1 egg white
- 1 ½ tbsp parsley (finely chopped)
- 1 tbsp mint (finely chopped)
- 2 garlic cloves (finely chopped)
- 1 tsp red chili sauce
- 1 tsp cayenne pepper
- 1 tsp coriander/ cilantro (ground)
- 1 tsp cumin (ground)
- 1 tsp salt

For Mint Yogurt

- 120ml / ½ cup of non-fat Greek yoghurt
- 60g / ¼ cup sour cream
- 15g / 1/10 cup of mint (finely chopped)
- 1 garlic clove (finely chopped)
- 2 tbsp buttermilk
- 2 pinches salt

METHOD

1. Preheat air fryer to 200°C / 392°F

2. Combine all the meatball ingredients in a large bowl

3. Roll the meatballs between the palms of your hands in a circular motion to make smooth golf ball sized meatballs

4. Place half of them into the air fryer basket and cook for 8 minutes

5. Repeat with the remaining meatballs

6. As the meatballs cook in the air fryer, mix the mint ingredients in a bowl, and serve alongside the hot meatballs

AIR FRIED CHEESEBURGERS

SERVES 4. CALORIES – 821, FAT – 47G, PROTEIN - 54G, CARBS – 42G
PREP TIME: 5 MINUTES. COOKING TIME: 20 MINUTES.

INGREDIENTS

- 450g / 15.8 oz. minced beef
- 4 hamburger buns
- 4 slices cheddar cheese
- 2 garlic cloves (crushed)
- Mayonnaise
- Lettuce
- Red onion (thinly sliced)
- Tomatoes (sliced)
- 1 tbsp soy sauce
- 1 pinch black pepper

METHOD

1. Put beef, soy sauce and crushed garlic together in a large bowl
2. Shape the beef into 4 burgers, then flatten them into 11cm patties
3. Season both sides of the patties with salt
4. Put 2 burgers into the air fryer and cook at 180°C / 356°F for about 4 minutes
5. Turn it and cook the opposite sides for around another 4 minutes
6. Repeat this process for the other 2 burgers
7. Spread mayonnaise on the hamburger buns
8. Add lettuce, then place the burgers inside
9. Top the tomatoes and onions, then cover with the other bun

SPICY FISH TACOS WITH SLAW

SERVES 4. CALORIES – 877, FAT – 42G, PROTEIN – 38G, CARBS – 87G
PREP TIME: 15 MINUTES. COOKING TIME: 20 MINUTES.

INGREDIENTS

- 360g / 12.6 oz. mahi mahi fillets
- 1.5kg / 3.3lbs green cabbage (shredded)
- 6-inch flour tortillas
- 125g / 1 cup of breadcrumbs
- 60g / ½ cup of flour
- 60g / ½ cup of mayonnaise
- 30g / ¼ cup of carrots (shredded)
- 60ml / ½ cup of milk
- 2 scallions (chopped)
- 1 egg, beaten
- 1 lime, divided into wedges
- 2 tbsp Sriracha slaw
- 1 tbsp olive oil
- 2 tbsp rice vinegar
- 1 tsp chili powder
- 1 tsp sugar
- 1 tsp salt
- ½ tsp cumin (ground)
- ½ tsp black pepper

METHOD

1. Combine the mayonnaise, sugar, Sriracha slaw and rice vinegar in a large mixing bowl

2. Add the green cabbage, shredded carrots and chopped scallions

3. Mix well and toss to ensure all the vegetables are thoroughly seasoned with salt and pepper

4. Put the slaw in the fridge until the tacos are ready

5. In another clean bowl, combine the cumin powder, flour, chili powder, pepper, salt, and baking powder

6. Add egg and milk and mix well to get a smooth batter

7. Place the breadcrumbs in a shallow dish

8. Slice the fish fillets into 2.5cm sticks

9. Toss the fish fillet sticks in the smooth batter to coat it

10. Let the excess drip off before dipping them into the breadcrumbs

11. Set the coated fish fillet stick on a baking tray and then coat all the other fish fillets in the same way

12. Preheat the air fryer to 200°C / 392°F

13. Spray the coated fish fillet sticks with olive oil

14. Place all the sticks in a single layer in the cooking basket, but be sure to leave some space around every stick

15. Air fry the coated fish fillet sticks for about 3 minutes, then turn them

16. Air fry for 2 more minutes

17. Warm your tortilla shells wrapped in foil in a 175°C / 347°F oven

18. If you prefer, you can also warm them in a skillet with a little oil over medium-high heat for around 2-3 minutes

19. Fold the tortillas in half and make your tacos by wrapping two air-fried coated fish fillet sticks in the tortilla shells

20. Top them off with the Sriracha slaw and squeeze lime juice over the top just before serving

CHEESE SOUFFLÉ

SERVES 5. CALORIES – 238, FAT – 12G, PROTEIN – 12G, CARBS – 15G
PREP TIME: 15 MINUTES. COOKING TIME: 30 MINUTES.

INGREDIENTS

- 4 whole eggs
- 60g / ½ cup of cheddar cheese
- 60g / ½ cup of all-purpose flour
- 30g / ¼ cup of panko breadcrumbs
- 350ml / 1 ½ cups of milk (skimmed is best for this)
- 30g / ¼ cup of butter
- 30g / ¼ cup of parmesan cheese (grated)
- 2 tbsp olive oil
- 2 tbsp fine white sugar
- ½ tbsp vanilla extract
- ½ tbsp nutmeg

METHOD

1. Preheat the air fryer to 167°C / 332°F

2. Grease the soufflé dishes with olive oil spray

3. Sprinkle the breadcrumbs on the greased dishes

4. Melt the butter in a small saucepan

5. Add in the all-purpose flour and stir the two ingredients together until smooth

6. Pour the mixture into a small, clean bowl and clean the saucepan

7. Heat the skimmed milk and then add the vanilla extract, stirring well

8. Bring the milk and vanilla extract to boil

9. Add the flour and butter mixture back into the pan

10. Whisk the ingredients together, making sure there are no lumps, until you have achieved a smooth consistency

11. Simmer the sauce to thicken it, then quickly suspend the saucepan over a bowl of iced water and let it cool for 10 minutes

12. Separate the egg whites from the egg yolks in a mixing bowl

13. Add the egg yolks to the thickened sauce, then stir in the parmesan and cheddar cheese

14. Sprinkle in the nutmeg for seasoning

15. Whisk up another batch of egg whites in a separate bowl until it forms soft peaks

16. With a metal spoon, stir the egg whites gradually into the sauce mixture

17. Divide the mixture evenly between the soufflé dishes, then use a knife to even out the tops

18. Place the soufflé dishes into the air fryer basket and set the timer for 20 minutes

19. When cooked, remove from the air fryer

20. Sprinkle some fine sugar across the top to serve

MAPLE AND MUSTARD- GLAZED TURKEY BREAST

SERVES 4. CALORIES – 413, FAT – 9G, PROTEIN - 73G, CARBS – 8G
PREP TIME: 5 MINUTES. COOKING TIME: 60 MINUTES.

INGREDIENTS

- 1.8kg / 3.9lbs whole turkey breast
- 60ml / ¼ cup of maple syrup
- 1 tbsp butter
- 2 tbsp Dijon mustard
- 2 tsp olive oil
- 1 tsp thyme (dried)
- ½ tsp sage (dried)
- ½ tsp paprika (smoked)
- ½ tsp black pepper
- A pinch of salt

METHOD

1. Preheat the air fryer to 175°C / 347°F

2. Brush the turkey breast with olive oil

3. Mix the dried sage, smoked paprika, dried thyme, black pepper, and salt together

4. Rub this mixture of spices over the turkey breast to season

5. Put the turkey breast into the cooking basket and cook in the air fryer for 25 minutes

6. Turn the turkey breast on its side inside the air fryer and cook for a further 12 minutes, then turn it onto the opposite side and cook it for 12 more minutes

7. Put the maple syrup, Dijon mustard and butter in a small saucepan and combine well, to make a nice glaze

8. Turn the turkey breast into an upright position in the air fryer and brush on the glaze

9. Cook for a final 5 minutes until it goes nicely brown

10. Let the turkey rest for about 5 minutes under a loose covering of aluminum foil before serving

AIR FRIED CHICKEN TENDERLOINS

SERVES 2. CALORIES – 125, FAT – 11G, PROTEIN – 26G, CARBS – 10G
PREP TIME: 5 MINUTES. COOKING TIME: 30 MINUTES.

INGREDIENTS

- 450g / 15.8 oz. chicken breast (tenders)
- 125g / 1 cup of panko breadcrumbs
- 2 large eggs
- 60g / ½ cup of parmesan cheese (finely shredded)
- 30g / ¼ cup of all-purpose flour
- 2 tbsp Italian seasoning
- 1 tsp garlic powder
- 1 tsp salt

METHOD

1. Combine the breadcrumbs, parmesan, garlic powder, Italian seasoning, and salt in a shallow dish

2. Pour the all-purpose flour into a separate shallow dish

3. Beat the eggs and pour them into third dish

4. Coat the chicken tenders in flour, shaking off any excess

5. Dip each flour-coated chicken tender into the beaten eggs

6. Let any excess drip off and roll them in the breadcrumb mixture

7. Put the coated chicken tenders in the air fryer, making sure that there is only one layer with a bit of space between each one

8. Cook at 150°C / 302°F for around 30 minutes

9. Take the chicken tenders out of the air fryer basket

10. Serve with your preferred dipping sauce

ROASTED VEGETABLE PASTA SALAD

SERVES 6. CALORIES – 37, FAT – 2G, PROTEIN – 1G, CARBS – 3G
PREP TIME: 5 MINUTES. COOKING TIME: 25 MINUTES.

INGREDIENTS

- 120g / 1 cup of mushrooms
- 90g / ½ cup of cherry tomatoes
- 450g / 15.8 oz. cooked penne pasta
- 90g / ½ cup of pitted olives
- 1 zucchini sliced into half-moons
- 1 squash (yellow) cut into half-moons
- 5 tbsp olive oil
- 1 orange bell pepper
- 1 green bell pepper
- 1 red pepper
- 1 red onion (sliced)
- 2 tbsp fresh basil
- 3 tbsp balsamic vinegar
- 1 tsp salt
- 1 tsp Italian seasoning
- ½ tsp black pepper

METHOD

1. Preheat air fryer to 193°C / 379°F

2. Put the red pepper, green pepper, orange pepper, zucchini, the yellow squash, mushrooms, and red onion in a large bowl

3. Add some olive oil and toss to coat the vegetables well

4. Season with salt, Italian seasoning, and black pepper

5. Air fry for 15 minutes in the cooking basket or until the vegetables become soften, but are not mushy

6. Stir when you are halfway through the cooking time to make sure the vegetables are all evenly roasted

7. Combine the cooked penne, olives, cherry tomatoes, and the roasted vegetables in another large bowl

8. Add the balsamic vinegar and toss well

9. Add some olive oil and stir to coat it all

10. Season with salt and black pepper

11. Put it in the fridge until you're ready to serve, then stir in the fresh basil and serve

AIR FRIED LEMON MAHI MAHI

SERVES 4. CALORIES – 91, FAT – 7G, PROTEIN – 5G, CARBS – 1G
PREP TIME: 5 MINUTES. COOKING TIME: 25 MINUTES

INGREDIENTS

- 180g / 6.3 oz. mahi mahi
- 2 tbsp butter
- Slices of lemon
- 1 tsp salt

METHOD

1. Wash and rinse the mahi mahi
2. Place the mahi mahi in a dish made of aluminum foil
3. Dress it with butter
4. Lay the lemon slices on top of the mahi mahi
5. Place the aluminum dish with mahi mahi into the air fryer basket
6. Slide the basket into the air fryer and cook at 175°C / 347°F for approx. 15 minutes
7. Season to taste with salt

SUN-DRIED TOMATO STAKES WITH COUSCOUS

SERVES 6. CALORIES – 735, FAT – 40G, PROTEIN – 28G, CARBS – 62G
PREP TIME: 10 MINUTES. COOKING TIME: 40 MINUTES.

INGREDIENTS

- 450g / 15.8 oz. steak
- 195g / 2 cups of dried lemon and hazelnut couscous
- 300ml / 1 cup water
- 95g / 1/3 cup of sun-dried tomatoes
- 120ml / ½ cup (approx.) of red wine vinegar
- 60ml / ¼ cup olive oil
- 25g / 0.8 oz. toasted hazelnuts (chopped)
- 30g / 0.9 oz. fresh parsley (chopped)
- 1 garlic clove (sliced)
- 2 tbsp fresh oregano
- 1 tbsp lemon zest (freshly chopped)
- 1 tbsp lemon juice
- 1 tbsp butter
- ½ tsp black pepper (ground)
- ½ tsp salt

METHOD

1. Cut the steak into pieces that you can put into your air fryer

2. Blend the sun-dried tomatoes with the fresh oregano into a paste using a blender

3. Add the red wine vinegar and ¼ of the olive oil and pulse again

4. Put the marinade paste into a re-sealable plastic bag

5. Add the black pepper and the clove of garlic

6. Use a tenderizer to tenderize the steak, you can pierce it several times with a paring knife

7. Take the steak and put it in the plastic bag containing the marinade paste and leave it to marinate for anywhere between 2 and 24 hours, in the fridge

8. 30 minutes before cooking, remove the steak from the bag

9. Preheat the air fryer to 200°C / 392°F

10. Season the marinated steak with salt and ground black pepper

11. Place the steak into the cooking basket and cook in the air fryer for 10 minutes, turning it after the first 5 minutes

12. Prepare the lemon and hazelnut couscous whilst the steak is cooking

13. First, put the dried couscous, lemon zest and a pinch of salt in a bowl

14. Pour 150ml / ½ cup of the boiling water into the bowl and stir once, then put the lid on

15. After 5 minutes, remove the lid and fluff the couscous with a fork

16. Add the tablespoon of butter, parsley, chopped hazelnuts and lemon juice

17. Remove from the air fryer and leave it to cool for 5 minutes before serving

Bonus Recipes: Snacks and Desserts

Are you searching for a little something you could air fry quickly to stave off hunger pangs in the gaps between meals? Are you wondering what desserts you could cook in your air fryer to help satiate your incurably sweet tooth? Never fear! We've got you covered. Read on to find some delicious snacks, as well as a selection of sugary, decadent desserts which you, your family, and friends can all enjoy.

Without further ado, let's dig into the bonus recipes.

Snacks

Here are some super tasty crowd-pleasing snacks you can air fry to perfection.

CRISPY POTATO SKINS

SERVES 4. CALORIES - 129, FAT – 5G, PROTEIN – 2G, CARBS – 19G
PREP TIME: 30 MINUTES. COOKING TIME: 30 MINUTES.

INGREDIENTS

- 6 medium-sized potatoes
- 2 tbsp of olive oil
- 1 tsp of paprika
- A pinch of salt
- A pinch of black pepper

METHOD

1. Scrub the potatoes under running water to clean them

2. Boil the potatoes in salted water for about 40 minutes until you can put a fork into them

3. Take the potatoes out of the boiling water and cool completely

4. You can put them in the fridge for a while to do this

5. Combine the paprika, olive oil, salt, and black pepper in a bowl

6. Chop the now cool potatoes into wedges and toss them in the seasoning mixture

7. Preheat the air fryer to 200°C / 392°F

8. Place half of the wedges into the fryer basket skin side down, making sure to leave some space around each one

9. Cook for 15 minutes, then repeat the process with the rest of the wedges

GARLIC ROASTED MUSHROOMS

SERVES 3. CALORIES – 92, FAT – 4G, PROTEIN – 7G, CARBS – 2G
PREP TIME: 5 MINUTES. COOKING TIME: 30 MINUTES.

INGREDIENTS

- 1kg / 2lbs of dried mushrooms
- 1 tbsp of duck fat
- 2 tbsp of herbs de Provence
- 2 tbsp of Vermouth
- ½ tbsp of garlic powder

METHOD

1. Wash the mushrooms and pat them dry with kitchen paper

2. Cut them into quarters and set them aside

3. Preheat the air fryer to 175°C / 347°F

4. Put the goose fat into the air fryer, adding the garlic powder and herbs de Provence

5. Heat for 2 minutes

6. Stir with a wooden spoon to eliminate clumps and add the mushrooms

7. Cook for 20 minutes

8. Add the Vermouth and cook for 5 more minutes before serving

ONION RINGS

SERVES 2. CALORIES - 581, FAT – 7G, PROTEIN – 23G, CARBS – 105G
PREP TIME: 5 MINS. COOKING TIME: 7 MINUTES.

INGREDIENTS

- 125g / 1 cup all-purpose flour
- 170g / 1½ cups panko breadcrumbs
- 1 medium-sized white onion (halved)
- 2 large eggs (beaten)
- 1 tsp paprika
- ½ tsp onion powder
- ½ tsp garlic powder
- A pinch of cayenne pepper
- A pinch of salt
- A pinch of black pepper (ground)
- Marinara sauce, to serve with

METHOD

1. Preheat the air fryer to 190°C / 375°F

2. Whisk the flour, paprika, onion powder, cayenne pepper, garlic powder, salt and pepper together in a bowl

3. Put the panko breadcrumbs and the 2 beaten eggs into separate bowls

4. Coat the onion rings in the flour, then in the eggs, then in the breadcrumbs

5. Put the onion rings in the air fryer basket in a single layer and set the timer for between 5 and 7 minutes until they go golden brown

6. Serve hot with marinara sauce

ROSEMARY POTATO CRISPS

SERVES 3. CALORIES – 120, FAT – 3G, PROTEIN – 2G, CARBS – 20G
PREP TIME: 5 MINUTES. COOKING TIME: 40 MINUTES.

INGREDIENTS

- 2 medium-sized potatoes
- 1 tbsp of olive oil
- 1 tsp of rosemary (chopped)
- A pinch of salt

METHOD

1. Scrub the potatoes under running water to clean them
2. Peel the potatoes and cut them lengthwise, then put them into a bowl of water
3. Soak the potato slices for 30 minutes, changing the water periodically
4. Drain them and pat dry with kitchen paper
5. Preheat the air fryer to 167°C / 332°F
6. Put the potatoes in a bowl and mix with olive oil
7. Place them in the air fryer cooking basket and let them cook for 30 minutes until golden brown
8. Shake at intervals to ensure even cooking
9. Toss the crisps into a bowl and mix them with salt and rosemary to serve

AIR FRIED SCONES

SERVES 6. CALORIES – 219, FAT – 8G, PROTEIN – 5G, CARBS – 32G
PREP TIME: 10 MINUTES. COOKING TIME: 7 MINUTES.

INGREDIENTS

- 225g / 7.9 oz. self-raising flour
- 28g / ¼ cup of caster sugar
- 50g / 1.7 oz. butter
- 60ml / ½ cup (6 tbsp) of milk
- Egg wash
- Olive oil spray (extra virgin is best)
- Strawberry jam to serve

METHOD

1. Put the sugar, flour, and butter together in a bowl

2. Rub the flour into the butter

3. Add milk until you can combine it into a soft dough

4. Flour a worktop and then roll the dough out on to it, the dough should be around 1.5cm thick

5. Cut out your dough into medium-sized scones using cutters

6. Place them in the air fryer basket

7. Spray the basket with the olive oil and apply the egg wash to the top of the scones

8. Cook the scones in the air fryer at 180°C / 360°F for 5 minutes

9. Turn the heat down and fry for 2 more minutes at 160°C / 320°F

10. Serve with strawberry jam

Serving suggestion: You could also serve with fresh slices of strawberry and fresh cream.

CRISPY AIR FRIED CHICKPEAS

SERVES 4. CALORIES – 251, FAT – 6G, PROTEIN – 1G CARBS – 36G
PREP TIME: 5 MINUTES. COOKING TIME: 15 MINUTES.

INGREDIENTS

- 538g / 19 oz. tin of chickpeas
- 1 tbsp olive oil
- ½ tsp paprika
- ¼ garlic powder
- ¼ tsp cayenne pepper
- A pinch of salt

METHOD

1. Preheat air fryer to 200°C / 392°F

2. Drain and rinse the chickpeas and mix them with the spices and olive oil

3. Put the chickpeas into the air fryer basket

4. Cook for between 12-15 minutes shaking the basket a few times to ensure even cooking

5. When the chickpeas are cooked enough for you and your family, remove them from the air fryer

6. Season to taste with salt and pepper

Desserts

Do you have a sweet tooth, or just enjoy your favourite chocolatey snack on occasion? Want more inspiration as to what sweet treats you can cook up in your air fryer? Remember, your new kitchen appliance is good for more than just making savory dishes and snacks.

Read on to find some delicious dessert recipes you can try out.

CHOCOLATE PROFITEROLES

SERVES 2. CALORIES – 390, FAT 27G, PROTEIN 7G, CARBS 45G
PREP TIME: 5 MINUTES. COOKING TIME: 20 MINUTES.

INGREDIENTS

- 125g / 1 cup of plain flour
- 6 medium–sized eggs (beaten)
- 110g / ½ cup of butter
- 2 tbsp icing sugar
- 2 tbsp vanilla essence
- 120g milk / ½ cup of milk chocolate
- 2 tbsp cream (whipped)

METHOD

1. Preheat the air fryer to 170°C / 338°F

2. Place ¾ of the butter into a pan over medium heat to bring it to boil

3. Take it off the heat and stir in the flour

4. Return it to the heat until it forms a dough

5. Set the dough aside and let it cool

6. Add the eggs and mix until you get a smooth consistency

7. Shape the dough into profiteroles and cook them in the air fryer for 10 minutes at 175°C / 347°F

8. Whisk the vanilla essence with icing sugar and whipped cream until nice and thick to make the filling

9. Prepare the chocolate topping by putting the milk chocolate, remaining butter, and cream into a bowl

10. Mix well over the heat to melt all the chocolate

11. Take the profiteroles from the air fryer and drizzle the chocolate sauce over them to serve

APPLE FRITTERS

SERVES 4. CALORIES - 100, FAT – 3G, PROTEIN – 2G, CARBS – 18G
PREP TIME: 10 MINUTES. COOKING TIME: 6 MINUTES.

INGREDIENTS

For the Fritters

- 2 apples, diced and cored
- 125g / 1 cup of all-purpose flour
- 2 tbsp sugar
- 1 tsp baking powder
- ½ tsp cinnamon (ground)
- A pinch of nutmeg
- 75ml / 1/3 cup milk
- 2 tbsp butter (melted)
- ½ tsp salt
- 1 egg
- ½ tsp lemon juice

For the cinnamon glaze

- 100g / ½ cup caster or granulated sugar
- 2 tbsp milk
- ½ tsp ground cinnamon
- A pinch of salt

METHOD

1. Dice the apples into small cubes and set aside, peel them if you prefer

2. Add the flour, sugar, baking powder, ground cinnamon, nutmeg and salt into a large bowl and stir to mix

3. In another bowl, combine the milk, butter, 1 egg, and lemon juice

4. Add the wet ingredients to the dry ingredients and stir until mixed

5. Stir in the apples, cover it, and put it all in the fridge for up to 2 days, for speed you can chill it for as little as 5 minutes

6. Preheat the air fryer to approx. 180°C / 360°F

7. Line the bottom of the fryer basket with baking parchment and scoop the apple fritter mixture into it, forming 2 tablespoon balls.

8. Slide the basket into the fryer and cook for 5-7 minutes

9. Meanwhile, whisk the cinnamon, milk, and salt together to create the glaze

10. Take the fritters out of the air fryer and transfer them to a wire cooling rack

11. Immediately pour the glaze over them and serve

CHOCOLATE BROWNIES

SERVES 3. CALORIES – 385, FAT – 18G, PROTEIN – 6G, CARBS – 54G
PREP TIME: 5 MINUTES. COOKING TIME: 20 MINUTES.

INGREDIENTS

- 160ml / ½ cup of milk (approx.)
- 170g / ¾ cup of brown sugar (approx.)
- 113g / ½ cup of butter
- 125g / just over ½ cup of caster sugar
- 60g / ½ cup of chocolate
- 120g / 1 cup of self-raising flour
- 2 bananas (sliced)
- 2 eggs (beaten)
- 2 tbsp vanilla essence
- 2 tbsp water

METHOD

1. Preheat the air fryer to 175°C / 347°F

2. Melt 3/4 of the butter and all of the chocolate in a bowl, over medium heat

3. Stir in the brown sugar, then add the beaten eggs and vanilla essence

4. Add the self-raising flour and mix well

5. Pour the dough into a greased dish and put it in the air fryer

6. Cook for 15 minutes

7. To make the caramel sauce mix the caster sugar and water in a saucepan over medium heat until the sugar melts

8. Turn up the heat and cook for 3 more minutes until the mixture goes a bit brown

9. Turn off the heat and let the sugar rest for 2 minutes before adding the rest of the butter and stir until it melts

10. Add the milk by mixing it in a little at a time

11. Take the caramel sauce, set it aside and let it cool

12. Remove the brownies from the air fryer and chop them into squares

13. Place them on a plate with sliced bananas and pour the caramel sauce over them before serving

AIR FRIED CHURROS

SERVES 6. CALORIES – 173, FAT – 10G, PROTEIN – 4G, CARBS - 17G
PREP TIME: 5 MINUTES. COOKING TIME: 20 MINUTES.

INGREDIENTS

- 60g butter / ¼ cup butter
- 120 ml / ½ cup milk
- 62g / ½ cup of all-purpose flour
- 2 eggs
- 50g / ¼ cup of white sugar
- ½ tsp cinnamon (ground)
- A pinch of salt

METHOD

1. Melt butter in a saucepan over medium-high heat

2. Pour in the milk and add salt

3. Turn the heat down to medium and bring it to boil, whilst stirring with a wooden spoon

4. Add the flour all in one go

5. Stir until the dough comes together

6. Take off the heat and leave to cool for around 5 minutes

7. Add the eggs to the mixture, stirring them in with a wooden spoon until the pastry forms

8. Put the dough into a piping bag with a large tip

9. Pipe the dough into strips in the air fryer basket

10. Fry the churros at 175°C / 340°F for 5 minutes

11. While the churros are in the air fryer, mix the sugar and cinnamon into a small bowl

12. Pour it into a dish

13. When the timer sounds on the churros, take them out and roll them in the sugar and cinnamon mixture

14. Serve warm

Serving suggestion: You could make a chocolate sauce or raspberry puree to serve alongside your churros.

PEANUT BUTTER AND MARSHMALLOW TURNOVERS

SERVES 4. CALORIES - 249, FAT – 8G, PROTEIN – 4G, CARBS – 41G
PREP TIME: 5 MINUTES. COOKING TIME: 20 MINUTES.

INGREDIENTS

- 4 sheets of filo pastry (defrosted)
- 4 tbsp peanut butter (chunky is best to add texture)
- 60g / ¼ cup of butter
- 4 tsp marshmallow fluff
- A pinch of sea salt

METHOD

1. Preheat the air fryer to 180°C / 356°F

2. Brush 1 sheet of filo with melted butter

3. Put the second filo pastry sheet on top of the first and brush it with butter again

4. Do the same for all the remaining sheets

5. Cut the filo layers into four 7cm x 30cm strips

6. Put 1 tablespoon of peanut butter and 1 teaspoon of marshmallow fluff on the underside of a strip of pastry

7. Fold the tip of the sheet over the filling and form a triangle and work in a zigzag pattern repeatedly until the filling is completely contained in the filo triangle

8. Seal the ends of the turnover with a dab of melted butter

9. Put the turnovers into the air fryer cooking basket and cook for between 3 and 5 minutes, until they turn golden brown and puff up a bit

10. Sprinkle with a pinch of salt before serving to create a delicious sweet and salty combination for all your friends and family to enjoy

AIR FRIED SHORTBREAD

SERVES 4. CALORIES – 635, FAT - 38G, PROTEIN – 9G, CARBS – 69G
PREP TIME: 10 MINUTES. COOKING TIME: 10 MINUTES

INGREDIENTS

- 250g / 8.8 oz. self-raising flour
- 175g / 6.1 oz. butter
- 75g / 2.6 oz. caster sugar

METHOD

1. Put the self-raising flour, butter, and caster sugar into a bowl

2. Rub the butter into the flour until it looks like thick breadcrumbs

3. Knead the dough until you have a dough ball, then roll out with a rolling pin.

4. Use cutters to cut out your preferred shapes

5. Cook your shortbread in the air fryer grill pan

6. Set the temperature to 180°C / 360°F and set the timer for 10 minutes

7. Leave them to cool on a wire rack before serving

CHEESECAKE CHIMICHANGAS

SERVES 4. CALORIES – 534, FAT – 28G, PROTEIN – 8G, CARBS – 64G
PREP TIME: 8 MINUTES. COOKING TIME: 10 MINUTES.

INGREDIENTS

- 226g / 8 oz. cream cheese (softened)
- 60g / ½ cup sugar (powdered)
- 1 tbsp of all-purpose flour
- 1 large egg
- ½ tsp vanilla extract
- 4 large flour tortillas
- 150g / 1 cup of cherry pie filling
- 50g / ¼ cup granulated sugar
- 1 tsp cinnamon (ground)
- 2 tbsp unsalted butter (melted)
- Olive oil spray

METHOD

1. Whisk the cream cheese in a medium-sized bowl until smooth

2. Add the powdered sugar and mix until well-combined

3. Add the egg, vanilla, and flower, mix until smooth

4. Preheat the air fryer to 182°C / 360°F

5. Put a tortilla on a clean work surface and put a quarter of the cheesecake mixture into the center of it

6. Top it off with a quarter of the cherry pie filling

7. Fold the bottom flap of the tortilla over the filling, ensuring that there is a flap to close the chimichanga

8. Fold the top flap of the tortilla over to form a little parcel

9. Spray the air fryer basket with olive oil spray

10. Put the tortillas into the basket seam side down, making sure they are not touching

11. Spray the tops with the olive oil

12. Air fry them for 8 to 10 minutes until they are golden brown

13. While waiting for the chimichangas to cook, put the cinnamon sugar on to a plate to mix

14. When the chimichangas are golden, brush them with melted butter

15. Finally, roll them in the sugar and cinnamon mixture and serve

AIR FRIED CHOCOLATE CHIP COOKIES

SERVES 4. CALORIES – 161, FAT – 8G, PROTEIN – 1G, CARBS – 21G
PREP TIME: 15 MINUTES. COOKING TIME: 7 MINUTES.

INGREDIENTS

- 14g / 1/8 a cup of sugar (granulated)
- 16g / 1/8 cup of brown sugar
- 1 ¾ tbsp butter
- 1 large egg
- 9g / 1/8 cup of rolled oats
- 27g / 1/5 cup + 2 tbsp of all-purpose flour
- A squeeze of lemon juice
- 1/2 tsp vanilla
- 78g / 1/3 cup of chocolate chips
- A pinch of baking soda
- A pinch of cinnamon
- A pinch of salt

METHOD

1. Combine the cream together with the butter and sugar in a large bowl, until well mixed

2. Add the egg, vanilla, and lemon juice and blend until it is light and fluffy

3. Mix the oats, flour, baking soda, salt and cinnamon in another large bowl

4. Add to the main mixture and mix for about 45 seconds to combine it well, taking care not to overmix

5. Stir in the chocolate chips with a spoon or spatula

6. Line the air fryer basket with foil, leaving space at the top and bottom edges of the basket for the are to move around the food

7. Scoop the dough into balls (about 2 tablespoons each) and place on foil, leaving 1 ½ to 2 inches between each ball of cookie dough

8. Lightly press the cookie dough down

9. Air fry at 149°C / 300°F for between 6-8 minutes

10. Lift the foil and cookies out of the air fryer

11. Let the cookies cool for about 5 minutes before placing them on a cooling rack for a further 5-10 minutes of cooling

12. Take care not to handle the cookies too soon, or they will crumble apart in your fingers

Conclusion

We hope you now feel confident enough to go fourth and fry up a storm for yourself, your friends, and your family with your XXL air fryer. You can use some of the simple, delicious recipes in this book as a starting point from which to embark on your personal air frying journey. As this book shows, you can use your new kitchen appliance to make moreish snacks and mouth-watering mains as well as several truly indulgent desserts. On top of all that, most of the dishes you'll create will be healthier versions of what you might have created using a deep fryer.

The versatility offered by the XXL air fryer gives you the ability to cook up 6 servings in one go. This — when combined with the multiple cooking options available to you — makes this the perfect fryer for you if you have a family or if you just enjoy entertaining friends.

Soon, with the help of this cookbook, you will be the talk of the town, impressing family, friends, and acquaintances with your new-found air frying prowess.

So, why wait? Buy a copy of this book today to take the first step on your personal culinary journey!

Disclaimer

This book contains opinions and ideas of the author and is meant to teach the reader informative and helpful knowledge while due care should be taken by the user in the application of the information provided. The instructions and strategies are possibly not right for every reader and there is no guarantee that they work for everyone. Using this book and implementing the information/recipes therein contained is explicitly your own responsibility and risk. This work with all its contents, does not guarantee correctness, completion, quality or correctness of the provided information. Misinformation or misprints cannot be completely eliminated.

Printed in Great Britain
by Amazon

73681211R00066